Paws & Claws

AN ANTHOLOGY OF CAT POETRY

In association with

THE CATS PROTECTION LEAGUE

HUTCHINSON

London Sydney Auckland Johannesburg

First published in 1995

1 3 5 7 9 10 8 6 4 2

© For this collection Hutchinson Children's Books 1995

© Text individual authors 1995

© Illustrations individual artists 1995

The individual authors and illustrators have asserted
their right under the Copyright, Designs and Patents Act, 1988,
to be identified as the authors and illustrators of this work

First published in the United Kingdom in 1995 by
Hutchinson Children's Books
Random House UK Limited
20 Vauxhall Bridge Road, London SW1V 2SA

Random House Australia (Pty) Limited
20 Alfred Street, Milsons Point, Sydney
New South Wales 2061, Australia

Random House New Zealand Limited
18 Poland Road, Glenfield
Auckland 10, New Zealand

Random House South Africa (Pty) Limited
PO Box 337, Bergvlei, South Africa
Random House UK Limited Reg. No. 954009

A CIP catalogue record for this book
is available from the British Library

ISBN: 0 09 176552 8

Printed in Belgium
by Proost International Book Production

Cover illustration: Reg Cartwright

CONTENTS

INTRODUCTION
by THE CATS PROTECTION LEAGUE

The Cats Protection League (CPL) was founded in 1927 by a group of concerned cat owners and breeders appalled by the number of unwanted cats and kittens found on the streets of London. The aims of the League were clearly defined and have remained unchanged since its foundation. They are:

1.   To rescue stray and unwanted cats and kittens, and to rehabilitate and rehome them where possible.
2.   To encourage the neutering of all cats and kittens not required for breeding.
3.   To inform the public on the care of cats and kittens.

Domino, May and September 1994,
rescued and restored to health by Tewkesbury, Twyning & District Group of The CPL

Photographs by kind permission of The Cats Protection League, Horsham

The League initially had its roots in London, but in the early 1930's it moved to Slough, where it remained until 1977. During these years, about twenty Groups and Branches run by unpaid volunteers were established dedicated to the welfare of cats, and the League's membership grew to about 4,000. An enforced move to Horsham in 1978 saw a dramatic increase in the number of Groups and Branches from seventy-six in 1980 to two hundred and thirty at the end of 1994. At the same time, membership of the League grew from 8,000 to 45,000 – a reflection of the League's growing position as the largest charity solely devoted to the welfare of cats. Every year, the League rescues and rehomes in excess of 70,000 cats and kittens, and neuters over 80,000. The League also has fourteen large Shelters run by Wardens, together with a small staff.

The bulk of the League's work is still done by its hard-working volunteers who are frequently referred to as the lifeblood of the charity – without their commitment, the League would not exist.

The Cats Protection League anticipates continued growth as we approach the end of the decade, reflecting the position of cats as the Number 1 domestic pet, and the League's prominence as the main cat charity.

There are still too many unwanted, ill-treated cats on our streets for the League to consider its work is done.

If you would like more information, please write to:
The Cats Protection League, 17 Kings Road,
Horsham, West Sussex, RH13 5PN.

A 14-Year-Old Convalescent Cat in the Winter

I want him to have another living summer,
to lie in the sun and enjoy the douceur de vivre –
because the sun, like golden rum in a rummer,
is what makes an idle cat un tout petit peu ivre –

I want him to lie stretched out, contented,
revelling in the heat, his fur all dry and warm,
an Old Age Pensioner, retired, resented
by no one, and happinesses in a beelike swarm

to settle on him – postponed for another season
that last fated hateful journey to the vet
from which there is no return (and age the reason)
which must soon come – as I cannot forget.

GAVIN EWART

Cat Began

Cat began.
She took the howling of the wind,
She took the screeching of the owl
And made her voice.

For her coat
She took the softness of the snow,
She took the yellow of the sand,
She took the shadows of the branches of the trees.

From deep wells
She took the silences of stones,
She took the moving of the water
For her walk.

Then at night
Cat took the glittering of stars,
She took the blackness of the sky
To make her eyes.

Fire and ice
Went in the sharpness of her claws
And for their shape
She took the new moon's slender curve –

And Cat was made.

ANDREW MATTHEWS

My Cat Shack

I called my cat Shack-Two.

Shack the First was a footballer.
Shackleton the Great,
Pride of Sunderland town.
Fleet of foot and lithe of limb,
With muscles that rippled as he ran
And hair that shone like silk.
Shack-One, my childhood hero,
The stuff of schoolgirl dreams.

But Shack-Two was my cat.
Every day, at 4 o'clock,
He'd meet me
Coming back from school,
High-stepping his way
Along the railings
That for me were shoulder-high.
And together, head to head,
We'd run along the street
That led to home, and milk
And toast for tea. And all the while
His blunt nose bumping against my face,
His rough tongue rasping on my cheek,
His purring noisy in my ear,
And his proud black plume of a tail
Writing exclamations of delight
In the air about me.

I loved him, my cat Shack,
When I was just a child.
I went back last year
To the street where once I lived,
And looked along the railings,

Waist-high now, remembering him,
And missing him.

And then he came, my memory-cat,
High-stepping his way towards me
From out of my childhood time,
Fleet of foot and lithe of limb,
With muscles that rippled as he ran,
And hair that shone like silk.
And his purring was like music
in my ear.

JENNIFER CURRY

Old Cat

For Gwenno, who's at least 19

Another winter dawn. I can't remember
how many mornings we've begun together,
me sipping tea, she lapping top-of-the-milk,
crunching munchies, licking her rusty silk.

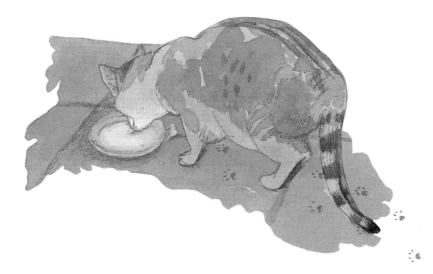

Like an old woman with a shabby coat
she dabs an old stain with a bit of spit,
combs her knots out with a tongue-washed paw,
then sits half-dreaming at the Rayburn door.

Old cat! Her walk is heavy now, and slow,
her coat is rough. One winter day I know
there may be no-one at the morning window,
only her paw-marks across fallen snow.

That morning, I'll switch on the kitchen light
and she won't leap to the sill out of the night,
her green eyes gleaming, silently mouthing 'O!
Let me in out of the wind and snow!'

But here she is again with a cry at the door.
I open it a crack to wind and sleet
and a handful of flakes. She delicately shakes each foot
and prints her daisy-chain across the floor.

Kettle and cat and stove will doze together,
adjusting old hearts to the icy weather.
All day the house will simmer with her purr,
like a loaf rising, the lift and fall of fur.

GILLIAN CLARKE

Sophisticat

Oliver Oliver Tortoiseshell
Quit his home at Dingley Dell
Where he had gone to no one was sure
Till he sent us a card from the Cote d'Azur
There you may see him every day
Strolling the Promenade des Anglais
Tips his hat and winks an eye
To society ladies passing by
His cane's malacca his tie just so
His suits handmade on Savile Row
Never was seen such a transformation
Never such feline sophistication.

Yet in one respect he remains as before
For when hunger strikes him at quarter to four
To the Café de Paris he'll repair
To claim his favourite table where
He takes a breath then raises his head
And howls and meowls until he gets fed.

GARETH OWEN

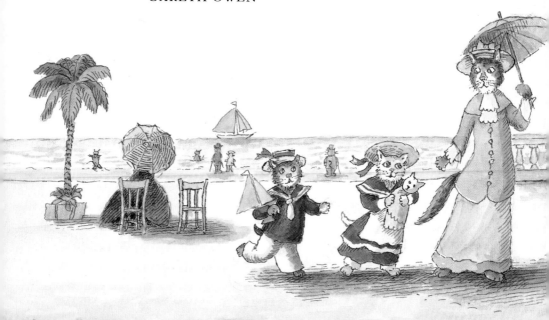

The Staff Room Cat

In the dingy Staff Room of a school in the city
    Where the teachers' damp macs hang limply from hooks,
Where cracked cups are tea-stained, the worn carpet gritty,
    And where there are piles of exercise books,
You will notice – at break – that the teachers don't utter
    A sound: none of them grumble and none of them chat.
Why? They dare not disturb what sleeps, fat as butter,
    On the Staff Room's best chair: one huge tortoiseshell cat.
        For the teachers
        Know very well not to wake him,
        For they know that he's three parts not tame.
        He's a *wild* cat, a *wild* cat,
        A not-to-be-riled cat,
        He's the Tortoiseshell Cat with No Name.

It was drizzly December when the cat first appeared
    And took the French teacher's chair for his bed.
Now his scimitar claws in the Staff Room are feared,
    Oh yes, *and* the street-fighter's teeth in his head.
Once a day he is seen doing arches and stretches
    Then for hours like a furry coiled fossil he'll lie.
It's true that he's made all the staff nervous wretches.
    They approach… and he opens one basilisk eye.
        For the teachers
        Know very well not to stroke him,
        For they know that he'll not play the game.
        He's a *wild* cat, a *wild* cat,
        A not-to-be-riled cat,
        He's the Tortoiseshell Cat with No Name.

The Headmistress, the teachers, and all the school's cleaners
    Can't shift him with even a long-handled broom,
For the cat merely yawns, treats them all like has-beeners
    And continues to live in that dingy Staff Room.
When the French teacher tried to reclaim her armchair
    With a cat-cally, shriek-squally, 'Allez-vous-en!'
The cat gave a hiss, clawed the lady's long hair,
    And back to Marseille Madame Touff-Pouff has gone.
        For the teachers
        Know very well not to irk him,
        For they know that he's always the same.
        He's a *wild* cat, a *wild* cat,
        A not-to-be-riled cat,
        He's the Tortoiseshell Cat with No Name.

I once worked in that school and observed the huge creature's
    Habits as I sipped my cracked cup of weak tea.
I saw how he frightened and flummoxed the teachers,
    And how, every Friday, he'd one-green-eye me.
To appease him, each day we laid out a fish dinner
    Which the beast snaffled-up in just one minute flat
Then returned to his chair with a smirk – the bad sinner!
    It seems there's no way to be rid of that cat.

      For the teachers
      Know very well not to cross him,
      For they know that he's three parts not tame.
      He's a *wild* cat, a *wild* cat
      A not-to-be-riled cat

      (he can't *bear* to be smiled at),

      He's the Tortoiseshell Cat with No Name,
      With No name,
      He's the Tortoiseshell Cat with No Name.

WES MAGEE

The Cats Protection League

Midnight. A knock at the door.
Open it? Better had.
Three heavy cats, mean and bad.

They offer protection. I ask, 'What for?'
The Boss-cat snarls, 'You know the score,
Listen man and listen good

If you wanna stay in the neighbourhood,
Pay your dues or the Toms will call
And wail each night on the backyard wall.

Mangle the flowers, and as for the lawn
A smelly minefield awaits you at dawn.'
These guys meant business without a doubt

Three cans of tuna, I handed them out.
They then disappeared like bats into hell
Those bad, bad cats from the CPL.

ROGER McGOUGH

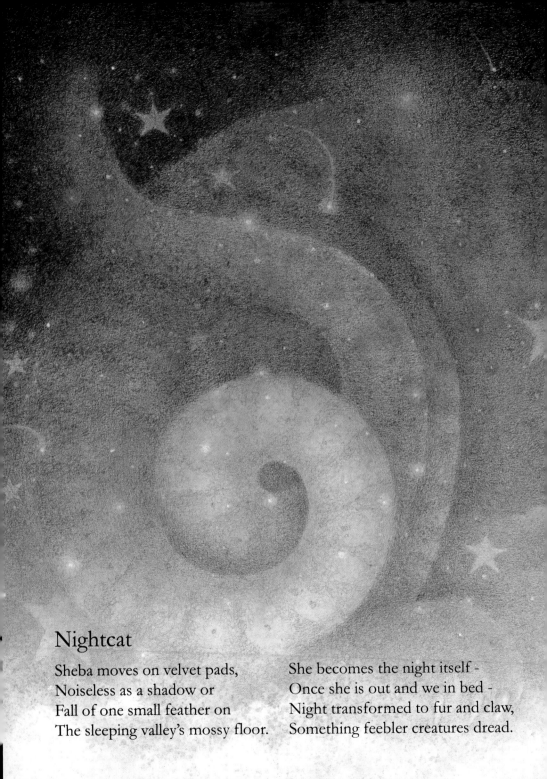

Nightcat

Sheba moves on velvet pads,
Noiseless as a shadow or
Fall of one small feather on
The sleeping valley's mossy floor.

She becomes the night itself -
Once she is out and we in bed -
Night transformed to fur and claw,
Something feebler creatures dread.

From her blackness, like two moons
In miniature, her eyes alone
betray her presence, gleaming bright
From where she crouches, still as stone.

But, at breakfast, we will find
Sheba on the carpet, curled,
Purring softly, tame and mild
In our human sunlit world.

VERNON SCANNELL

White Cat on a Frozen Pool

Silent as milk
From an ivory spool,
The white cat walked
The frozen pool.

Windless it was,
With hoar-frost laid;
Burned on the ice
The white cat's shade.

No eerier sight
Than how it froze
When through the ice
Suspended fish uprose,

And separated
By the winter-glass,
Cat over quarry
Magically passed.

PAULINE STAINER

A Cat Like That

He haunts the graveyard –
A tomb-grey, silent tom
Who steals on moss-soft pads
Between the lichened stones.
They say he has no voice –
No miaow or yowl,
No purring rumble
When he's fed and warm;
They say he's not like other cats
At all.

But I don't think that many
Know this old cat like I do!
I don't think they've
Glimpsed him, fading
At dusk down narrow pathways,
Sweet as wandering wood-smoke…
Drifting… gone…
And I don't think they've found
His downy hollow,
Deep in the shady corner where
The yew tree sighs
And nettles and long grasses close
Over forgotten secrets
No-one knows.

They say he must be sad,
A cat like that,
A graveyard cat who's seen sad sights –
But they have never watched him
Whirling,
Misty, will-o' the-wisp-y,
Round the wind-worn headstones
At first light.

And only I,
One starry, snowswept Christmas,
Saw him at midnight once,
Inside the church, as we were
On our knees.
Over the icy flags he skipped,
Spangled with hoar,
And with his amber eyes
As round and bright
As candlelight!

GINA WILSON

Unkind, Ungrateful

Blackie my cat is looking at the back door.
I say Here, puss
    a plea which – as usual –
    he chooses to ignore.

Today, he has
(A) pulled a hank of hair
    out of the neck of a neighbour's cat,
    and not content with that,
(B) he has walked on a painted chair
    and trailed paint everywhere.

(C) He has disgraced himself – twice –
    on the lettuces,
    knowing perfectly well that peed-on lettuces are not nice.

(D) He has scalped a magpie, and scattering
    most of its feathers over the lawn, come pattering
    here to the kitchen with it, pretending it was an offering.

I happened to be cooking a chicken at this point, so bang
                             went my appetite.
His dead bird made mine seem not so much disgusting as
                                just not right.

Now he turns his back and stares at the back door.
Plainly I bore him. He would prefer to go out and explore,
    now that his patient pink tongue has licked the last trace
    of chicken fat from his whiskery face.

I wish he were kinder and not quite so rude
    but there is no bottom, none, to cats' ingratitude.

IAN WHYBROW

Bing Bong, the Rolling Cat

Suppose your tummy was as big and round
as my cat Bing Bong's is. You'd have to think
before you settled in a chair or found
the perfect place to have your forty winks.
Some spots would be too dangerous, in case
you rolled around while sleeping and became
a wandering fur ball, rolling any place –
for instance, right into a football game.
But Bing Bong likes the kitchen table best
for snoozing, when we gather round for meals.
He tucks his paws in tight beside his chest
and rolls among our plates as if on wheels.
    Oh no! Too far! He's landed on the floor.
    The table's not his bedroom anymore.

LINDA CHASE

Purr

And the purr starts up
regular as an engine, vibrating
in its throat, racking its body
you can see all the tremors –
and soon it purrs outside its fur.
Then the purr is free-ranging
cruising around the room
creeping into patterns in the rug
loud as a burst of sun
haunting as a burst of night.
The whole room waits for you to purr.
A whiff of purr, and then a grand purr
and now you're rumbling so much
you can hardly breathe
with lovers' purr and artists' purr
builders' purr and actors' purr
athletes' purr and electricians' purr
the found child's purr
the first purr
and the last purr

MONIZA ALVI

```
              ∧                       K
      E       C               R       C
  H           A           A           A
  T           R           P           T
```

Car bonnet cat
keeping warm, car bonnet cat
with crocodile yawn, stares from his sand-
peppered forest of fluff, segment-of-lemon eyes warning,
ENOUGH!   Just draw back that hand, retreat,   *GO AWAY!*
and his claws flex a tune to say: I won't play but I'll spit
like the sea whipped wild   in a gale,   hump up like a wave,
flick a forked lightning tail,   lash out and scratch at
your lobster-pink face, for no one, *but no one*,
removes from this place, car bonnet cat
keeping warm,   car bonnet cat
by the name of
STORM .

GINA DOUTHWAITE

For She Is Pursued by Shadows

The sun creeps towards me across six gardens.
The ginger cats perch here and there,
marking the slothful hours.

I always feel better at this time of day,
when the sun falls on the bird table
and the cats are preening themselves on the walls.

The days are circular. Smiling or hungry,
the cats sit in them, indicating the passage of time
by the position of a tail.

The distrustful Siamese who never purrs
slinks down the wall on her belly,
running some private gauntlet with the sun,
her ears pinned back.
She it was who devoured all her kittens.

HUGO WILLIAMS

Smoke

Since you died, this grey stranger
comes daily to my garden: shadow-cat
curled on grass, where the low-slanting
sun barely reaches. He grows greyer

and greyer. As the year's leaves
turn to ash, as the flames fatten
and crack, I see him fading
into smoke, his eyes, nose, tongue,

all the delicate small bones of him
half-buried in grey fur, as if waiting
for a shadow-hand to stroke sparks
from his coat, and pass through him.

SUSAN WICKS

The Cat With No Name

The cat with no name
is a shadow that flits by the back of the barn.

The cat with no name
slips out by the gate at the edge of the farm.

The cat with no name
goes unseen by the lights of the cars in the lane.

While the dog in the yard
dreams a ghost has walked over its chain.

The cat with no name
has eyes like two lemon moons that narrow and dim.

The cat with no name
has no home but the night that's a part of him.

The cat with no name
trusts no-one and wants no trust.

The cat with no name
is as dark as a thought you had (or you thought you had)

that got lost.

STUART HENSON

Mid-Life Crisis

Once I lived in a red brick house
Where, wintertimes, I basked in the glow
Of a big coal fire. And Jenny would bring me
Jellied meat, and milk in a saucer.

But I grew tired of Kitty Katt
At 8 a.m. and 6 p.m.
And little Jane pulling my tail
As if I were her teddy bear.

One day I ran away:
I followed the asphalt road,
Pounding the ground with swelling paws,
Till I reached the forest shade.

Here I hunt for robins and thrushes,
Spring water I drink from a running stream
My home's the forest.
This indeed is *living*.

MICHAEL CULHANE

Raining Cats and Dogs…

If it really did rain cats and dogs,
I wonder how they'd all get on?
Would the cats just hex their old rivals,
hissing at them to be gone?

Would the dogs start chasing their tails
instead of the scowling cats,
or would they bark at other things that moved
such as birds and long-eared bats?

Would there be a storm of collisions
as it got busier and busier up there,
with sky pounding, pounding cats and dogs
and all coming up for air?

Would they turn the day bark-hiss-inside-out,
would they suddenly go quite crazy,
or would they just doze their whole way down
and enjoy being rain-sleep lazy?

KATHERINE GALLAGHER

My Cat Really Digs Me

If, as I write
This rhyme tonight,
Something should cause
My pen to pause,
It's not that I'm
Bereft of rhyme,
But rather that
My sleepy cat
Lies on my lap
Taking a nap,
And on his paws
Are great big claws
Which dig deep in
My tender skin
Until I must
His feet adjust,
As now, indeed,
I feel the need
To do, so I'll
Just pause awhile
. . . .
. . . .
That's better, I'm
Now fit to rhyme!

COLIN WEST

Marmalade

He's buried in the bushes
with dock leaves round his grave,
a crime cat desperado
and his name was Marmalade.
He's the cat that caught the pigeon
that stole the neighbour's meat...
and tore the velvet curtain
and stained the satin seat.
He's the cat that spoilt the laundry
he's the cat that spoilt the stew
and chased the lady's poodle
and scratched her daughter too.

But –
no more we'll hear his cat-flap
or scratches at the door
or see him at the window
or hear his catnap snore.

So –
ring his grave with pebbles
erect a noble sign.
For here lies Mr Marmalade
and Marmalade was *mine*.

PETER DIXON

Trespussing

Excuse me, but please would you move from my bed?
I have told you again and again.
I don't know how often it has to be said:
You're a pussy and I'm a Great Dane.

You've got your own basket. It's over there. See?
It's the small one that's next to the sink.
When I ask you to shift I expect you to go
And not to just sit there and blink.

My mistress and I have come back from our walk
And I don't mind admitting I'm whacked.
I want to lie down. Are you deaf? Are you blind?
Are you getting a cat cataract?

I can't possibly fit into *your* little bunk
And don't think for a moment I'll try.
You're a dog in the manger with all of this space –
Now don't be a nuisance. Shoo-fly!

The trouble with you and the rest of your ilk
Is your self-possessed, indolent pose.
The last time you did this to me, I recall,
You spat at me, then scratched my nose.

I've heard people say that in fact you're a stray
And they found you in some kind of slum.
Well, I'm one up on *you* for my blood's royal blue.
Yes I am a pedigree, chum.

You're the laziest, lousiest cat I have met.
Every dog that I know would concur.
You are not at all nice, you can't even catch mice
But just sleep and eat, scratch things and purr.

I've had quite enough, so just listen! Ruff! Ruff!
Grrr! Harooo! You heard what I said.
I will bark in your face till you're in your own place.
For the last time, GET OUT OF MY BED!
*   *   *   *   *   *   *

Now *I'm* in the dog-house for making a noise,
You over-fed, under-bred brat.
Dear oh dear, the indignity I must endure
Of cohabiting here with a cat.

But every Great Dane has his day, as they say
And it's worth every minute, by heck,
When the mistress comes in and without further ado
You're thrown out by the scruff of your neck!

JEREMY NICHOLAS

The Presbytery Cat

As a joke, they would call him
Beelzebub:

a shadow that flared in the curtains
when passing headlamps swept across the room,

a prodigal, home from the rooftops,
perched at an upstairs window

like old Grimalkin.
A neighbour had moved and left them
this devil with one white paw,

a holy terror, burgling the fridge
to steal their fish on Friday afternoons,

then bringing them mice and songbirds,
in part-exchange,

or crossing The Herald, laid on the kitchen floor,
and leaving a trail of perfectly detailed claws.

A name, once given, cannot be withdrawn,
but sometimes they wished they had called him

Peter, or John the Baptist,
Bartholomew, Simon, Lazarus, Nicodemus,

or Thomas, after the one
who doubted, then wandered away

in legend, to begin another church
somewhere between Damascus and Ceylon.

JOHN BURNSIDE

Good Bad Cat

O cat,
Cat on the mat,
What did you do this morning?
Did you prim your fur
With a languid purr,
Twitching your tail and yawning?
Did you spread your all
On the garden wall
Which is horribly high,
But you never fall –
Sleepily blinking, lazily winking
Your amber eyes with the luminous twinkling?

O cat,
Fat on the mat,
Where have you been since lunch,
When you had your fish
In your own small dish –
Gobble and gulp and crunch?
Did you creep upstairs
Leaving ginger hairs,
To your favourite couch
Where the laundry airs?
Snugged in the dresses, knickers and vestses,
Comfortably plump, my prince of pestses.

O cat,
Flat on the mat
How do you spend your nights?
Do you sing sweet airs
To the wheeling stars
Squat on a height of heights?
Do you crouch and croon
To the giddy moon
That hangs in the dark
Like a silver spoon?
Crazy starer, yellow-eyed glarer,
Electrical spectacle. Heart ensnarer.

JOSEPHINE POOLE

Daft as a Shipyard Cat

There's nowt as daft as a shipyard cat
Sent mad by shipbuilding machinery.
Wanders wild from dry dock t'quay
Spends days stalking 'twen metal flays.
Larks dodging sparks from welder's arcs
Fed on scraps; naps in docker's caps
Sits snug like an overseer.
Venerable it watches; scratches;
Smirks at men at work.
Best known in yards on Tyne and Wear.
Now shipyard's gates are finally closed
What'll 'appen to cat… and men?
Na body knows.

KEL HIBBERD

Fred

The wind gently lifts a clump of matted fur.
The only thing to distinguish you
from a scrap of rain-sodden carpet
is when you turn your head
and I catch a glimpse of your one golden paw.

MARGI BATES

Viking Cat

When Viking longships cut seas
like ploughs turning the fields,
wave wanderers
on the lip of the sea's thunder,

the Viking cat curled in a longship's stern
her black fur pointed with foam,
her tart triangular face hidden
safe from the waves' claws and the drench of salt.

Men and the water roared at each other,
the sharp-toothed waves were hungry to swallow
the black smudge of the Viking cat
but she turned her back on them and slept.

On the holy island of Lindisfarne
monks and villagers also lay sleeping.
They did not dream of grey ghosts crossing
the furrowed field of the sea towards them.

The dawn sea turned to a sunrise of blood.
The Viking cat with her back arched
followed the wave wanderers
as they split the air with the sea's thunder.

On the holy island of Lindisfarne
there is a walled garden
where honey bees make summer happen
in a music of murmuring,

and there you can find the Viking cat's
fifty times grand-daughter,
black fur sleek with the sun,
eyes shut, basking

where nectar simmers in horned thistles,
where the sea-wind never comes.
Now, she twitches. In dreams she's leaping
to catch a butterfly among the ruins.

HELEN DUNMORE

Aubade

I light the candle, fill the tub,
he joins me when he hears the swish
of displaced water.

We talk, at least I talk,
he listens, nods occasionally,
he bats the soap, the sponge, the plug;

he likes it when the baby kicks
sending the ripples through the surface
from a source that he can't see.

Often when he perches on the edge
his tail dips in the water
like a wick; he doesn't seem to mind,

perhaps he doesn't notice.
Eventually the heat releases both of us,
we sink into a stupor

and sometimes then I think
this is almost enough -
almost a family:

me, the cat, the unborn child.

KATIE CAMPBELL

'Oh No! Not Tinned Cat Food Again!'

They've given me cat food again!
That stuff from the tin that's marked CHEAP.
It tastes like the armpits of camels
Who died in the dunes in their sleep.

Can't they see it's not fit for consumption?
Don't they care that it's something I *hate*?
Are they not nonplussed by my look of disgust
And the way I back off from the plate?

What I'd give for the breast of a chicken
Or a succulent slice from the roast,
Or those jolly wee packets of crab sticks!
All those things that a moggy likes most.

Hey! A Cod-In-A-Bag from the freezer.
Now, that's what you call a good meal.
Or the turkey they gave me last Christmas.
(That was nine months ago now. Big deal.)

Errol next door lives on pilchards.
(I've seen him eat lobster as well.)
He sometimes – oh heaven – gets cream sent from Devon
While I get tinned camel from hell.

I do what I can to persuade them.
I wheedle, I plead and I beg.
I twine in and out of their ankles,
Try sinking my claws in their leg…

But no. They're determined to break me.
'Leave it down,' they all say. 'He'll give in.'
But I'd much sooner starve in a gutter
Than sample that muck from a tin.

So I'll strut from the kitchen with feeling,
And a sniff and a sneer and a swish,
And I'll leave that tinned cat food congealing
In little brown lumps on the dish.

I'll go out and sit in the garden,
And coldly stare down from the wall.
I'll turn a deaf ear to their coaxing,
I will not respond when they call.

I'll stay there all night if I have to,
All night and the following day.
And refuse to return 'til they finally learn
I DO *NOT* LIKE TINNED CAT FOOD! OKAY?

KAYE UMANSKY

Witch's Familiar

Working with witches is all very well,
If you can put up with the terrible smell.
The potions they make for each evil spell
Are so incredibly vile
That even my mistress gasps and chokes,
Ragwort the Raven flutters and croaks,
Only the skeletons smile.

But broomstick rides across night skies
Are a tricky treat I recognise.
It's wicked to be a black cat that flies –
A most agreeable purrk!
And the office can be paradise
When Malevola sleeps and I chase mice.
It's not all work.

I help my mistress all year long,
Making sure that right is wrong.
But, you know, this poisonous pong
Makes me want to spit.
Despite the fact I've grown quite rich,
Can classify which witch is which,
It's high time to quit.

Although this is a tempting wheeze,
There's someone that it would displease.
Black cats like me don't grow on trees,
And witches rule, OK…
Malevola needs her familiar friend,
Only a fool would recommend
That I should run away.

So think of me on Hallowe'en,
When school lunch makes your face turn green,
Or you get stuck in an old latrine:
Who would be a pet?
It's a dog's life, don't you think,
To live with this perpetual stink?
So please don't forget

That CPL spells a magic cause
Which brings a huge applause of paws.

PAUL SIDEY

Maffrey

Black Maffrey was a witch's cat,
And soared behind upon the broom,
Past trees, through clouds and chilling winds,
In secretive and gleeful gloom.

Sly Maffrey knew six hundred spells,
Gleamed from the witch's book at night,
Spells of Great Changings, love and hate,
Of thunderbolts and x-ray sight.

Poor Maffrey worked from dawn to dusk –
To do the bidding of the witch;
She swept her castle every day,
And scrubbed the curtains in the ditch.

She stitched the witch's tattered cloak,
She stacked the sacks of dragons' toes;
She beat the carpets free from dust,
And set the newtling jars in rows.

She worked until her paws were sore,
To make the witch's castle clean;
But never once was praised or thanked,
And ever earned a lick of cream!

'You must work harder,' cried the witch.
'No treats for lazy cats like you!'
So Maffrey twirled an angry tail –
And FLASH! the witch was purple goo!

Now Maffrey is a witch supreme,
And keeps a cat to clean and cook;
And Maffrey fills her cat with cream –
But never lets it read her book.

MICHAEL RATNETT

Cheese

Would someone kindly tell me, please
Whose paw prints are they, in the cheese?
'Not mine!' insists the Siamese,
'It must have been the Tabby.'
But would he stoop to crimes like these?
Not him. He may be full of fleas,
Despite his scars and scruffy knees
His morals are not shabby.

As for Madam! As for her,
That bag of nails wrapped in fur,
I don't believe a single purr,
She isn't fooling me.
Despite the twitching of her tail,
The innocence in every wail
Upon her whiskers ends a trail
Of Camembert and Brie.

JEANNE WILLIS

Purrfection, at Last

What a wonderful thing is the cat!
on making it God said, 'That's that!
Supurrnatural selection has brought us purrfection –

*which is a great relief to Me after My earlier mistake with the
nematode worm.'*

ROWENA SOMMERVILLE

Jack

I'm ready to go now,
Tired to the bone.
I miss my old place;
plenty of room and a garden.
I haven't seen the outside
since I moved here.
Anyway, there's nothing to see,
just tower blocks and the railway.
He's never home and my tray gets filthy,
then he shouts if I do it on the floor.
He lets me sleep on the bed,
unless he's brought a friend home.
There's one girl who used to come,
but she's not been here for awhile:
Deep voice and a big, big laugh.
I'm a bit scared of people, really.
He's all right,
but I know he only took me for his mum's sake.
Had to go into sheltered,.
So bad luck, Jack.
I'm ready to go now,
Tired to the bone.
I miss my old place.

CAROLINE COOKE